The Most Important Letter You Will Ever Write

How to Tell Loved Ones How You Feel –
Before It's Too Late

Lilia L. Fallgatter

Inspirit Books, LLC

Printed in the United States of America
10 Digit ISBN: 0-9776574-0-X
13 Digit ISBN: 978-0-9776574-0-7
Library of Congress: 2005910590

Cover design by Jose M. Espinoza,
Espinoza Graphics, Carmel, CA

Layout by J.L. Saloff
Saloff Enterprises, Edinboro, PA

Written requests for permission to make copies of any part of this work can be made to:

Inspirit Books
PO Box 13736
Chandler, AZ 85248
Fax: 480.895.3021
www.lovingletter.com

To Spencer, Alexandra, Kristian,
Adela and Manuel

for their endless love and support.

Acknowledgments

"Let no one seek his own, but each the other's well being."

1 Corinthians 10:24

There are many people who have helped me take this book from dream to reality. From those who participated in my first workshop, to those who have been there to lend a hand or an ear through the writing and publication of the book, these individuals have given of themselves so that I might benefit from their time and talents.

I would like to thank my family members, my husband (and captive audience) Spencer and my children, Alexandra and Kristian (my other passions) who have had to go without some of my time so that I might fulfill a dream. To my parents, Manuel and Adela Espinoza, who have loved and taught me well. To my siblings Marisa Espinoza, Diane Grijalva and Manny Espinoza, to whom I often turned for help, thank you all for being there.

Thanks to my friends, especially Analilia Saldivar and Joanne Stark, for their amazing grace and ability to see the positive side of anything. To the APME Workshop participants: Marisa Espinoza, Spencer Fallgatter, Joe Gregory, Diane Grijalva, Teresa Palmer, Analilia Saldivar, Pamela Samuels, Joanne Stark and Molly Wright; your time and honest feedback meant more than you will ever know. To the Serious Scribes writing group, especially Mitzi Kleidon and Srianthi Perera, for their support and encouragement. Thanks also to Tom Bird who, through his books and workshops, has inspired many (including me) to fulfill their writing dreams.

Thanks to my editors for their relentless pursuit of the grammatically incorrect and for their remarkably sharp minds and pens.

Finally, thanks to all of the beautiful souls who inspired the idea of Loving Letters. I offer my undying gratitude for lessons learned. Because you lived, my life is replete with knowledge and wisdom. Because you lived, my life is brimming with love and happiness. This world is better —because you lived.

Table of Contents

1.

Introduction

If you died tomorrow, would the people you love know how you felt about them?

In the course of a lifetime, there are many people who come in to and go out of our lives. Some are steadfast in their presence, others fleeting. Each serves a particular purpose or teaches a particular lesson. Those people – our loved ones, family members, friends and sometimes even perfect strangers – leave distinct imprints on the pages in the book of our souls. In the course of my lifetime, I have encountered several such individuals. Some have made a greater impact than others, but all are significant and have helped me to become the person I am today.

Many of these individuals have played a significant role in the uncovering of this book, which has long been hidden deep within me. The idea for writing this book emerged from my own need and desire to let people in my life know what they mean to me, and to do so in an effective and meaningful way. I'm not sure exactly why the desire arose, but I felt a sense of urgency. I felt I had to do it soon or it would be too late. Perhaps it came from being in my early 40's. Maybe it was because I had become more aware of relatives, friends and acquaintances being ill or dying. Whatever the reason, the need to communicate my feelings resulted in my developing the process for writing "Loving Letters" to loved ones.

The purpose of this book is to introduce that process; a way for communicating with loved ones in writing. As you might have guessed, Loving Letters are letters written to people we love or care about, telling them how we feel about them and why. The book is not intended to provide writing instruction. Instead, it describes the process and provides guidance for writing Loving Letters. The letters, however, are to be created by you and will be your unique works (words) of art.

Also included are detailed exercises, samples and resources. The exercises and samples are intended to take you step-by-step through the process and allow you to experience first-hand how easy it can be to communicate in writing with those you value most. The resources are included to provide guidance, motivation and inspiration.

My hope is that by following the steps for writing a Loving Letter you may:

> ➤ Communicate with all of the people you love, appreciate and who have had a positive impact on your life, but who may not know it.

●◆ Save yourself from the pain of regret that can result from things being left unsaid.

●◆ Answer the question posed at the beginning of this chapter with a resounding "YES."

As a reader, I know that a book has met or exceeded the author's purpose in writing it, if the reader believes she[1] is in some way a better person for having read it. My purpose in writing this book will have been met if only one person benefits from it.

In the pages that follow, you will discover why a Loving Letter may indeed be *"The Most Important Letter You Will Ever Write."*

---

1. Unless used in reference to a specific person, the terms "he," "she," "him" and "her" are used interchangeably.

2.

A Letter to Jen

Some things in life are far too important to put off. My letter to my friend Jen[2] was one of them.

When I learned from my sister, Marisa, that our friend had cancer, I was saddened by the news, but was optimistic that everything would be okay. In the months following her diagnosis, I spoke with Jen (who lived 100 miles away) by phone a few times and got regular updates from my sister.

Before traveling to a family reunion in June of 2003, Jen had taken a turn for the worse and was in the hospital. I remained hopeful. When we returned 11 days later, she was gone; a stunningly short 6 months following her diagnosis. I was deeply saddened by her death and felt badly that I had not made more of an effort to be there for Jen as she neared the end of her life. Even though she was gone, I decided to write Jen a letter telling her what she had meant to me.

---

2. Fictitious names may be used to protect individual privacy rights.

A Letter to Jen

Dear Jen,

I'm sorry I did not take the opportunity to say any of this while you were still with us to hear it. The last conversation we had by phone was so normal and natural and you seemed so very optimistic about the future. I admired your strength and resilience in the face of the unknown. I never imagined you would slip away from us so quickly. I never imagined I would never get to thank you and tell you how much I appreciated your friendship and graceful presence in my life.

I am thankful that your friendship with Marisa brought you into my life. Soon after I met you, I came to realize what a truly gentle and caring spirit you were. As Marisa's sister who had just moved to Phoenix in 1986, you took me in as your friend also and made me feel instantly at ease. Despite Marisa telling me to "get my own friends," when you called for her but talked to me, I enjoyed our conversations more than you'll ever know.

I'll never forget the great fun we had

playing poker. Sharing food and drinks, relaxation and conversation was a blast. Your love and dedication to your feline family and other friends in your life was an inspiration.

It seems that a good part of your mission in life was to be of service to others.

I want to thank you for being there for so many of the important events in my life: My marriage to Spencer, the birth of our two babies and on many other happy occasions. It meant a lot to us to have you there. Thank you for all of the genuine and loving support you offered over the years.

I miss you Jen, your talkative nature and your great sense of humor. I miss your loving and thoughtful ways.

All My Love,

Writing the letter telling my friend what she meant to me made me feel better. I'm not sure why exactly. Maybe it was because somewhere in the back of my mind, I believed my words would somehow transcend space and time and make their way to Jen, wherever she was. In reading and re-reading my letter to her, I felt a certain regret. I wondered why I had not taken the time to say or write these things to Jen before she died. How simple it would have been to do so; and how satisfying it would be to know that she knew how important she was to me. I wondered how many people across the country or around the world found themselves in similar situations and feeling the same kind of regret as they faced the loss of someone they loved.

People Die

Life is temporary. Though we are consciously aware of that fact, we live in a society in which we don't think about death until we are forced to do so. Focusing on mortality (whether our own or that of loved ones) can be beneficial, in that affords us the opportunity to reflect on the things that matter most. It allows us to examine our priorities and consider whether we are living our lives in a way that aligns with those things that are important to us.

Although we may like to think that we, and the people we love, will be around forever, the truth of course, is that we won't be. People die. In 2002 alone, over 2.4 million people died in the United States.[3] With annual deaths in

---

3. Data reported by the National Center for Health Statistics, Center for Disease Control.

such high numbers, imagine the even greater number of grieving loved ones left behind. What is the likelihood that some of those loved ones wondered if the person they lost really knew how much they were loved and possibly regretted not having told them? Based on numbers alone, it is safe to say it is very likely.

According to the many resources available (in print and on the internet) on the topic of grief, the bereaved deal with loss in a number of ways. Included among them are dealing with loss through writing and journaling. One book on grief notes that "[w]riting a letter to a loved one is a powerful tool."[4] In another, the author notes "[t]he bereaved report that writing letters to their deceased loved ones or journaling helps them vent their feelings and tie up loose ends."[5]

I refer to letters (or any communication) to deceased loved ones, such as my letter to Jen, as Post Mortem Expression (PME) because loved ones are no longer physically present to hear, appreciate or enjoy what we have to "say" to them. That is not to say that PME is not beneficial. As noted above, writing to deceased loved ones may help the bereaved cope with their loss, and therefore, serves a beneficial purpose. It certainly made me feel better to write a letter to my friend. In spite of that, I couldn't help but think about how simple it would have been for me to write the very same words before she died.

Loss of life occurs daily and for a number of reasons. It may be due to natural causes, illness or disease, murder,

---

4. *Five Cries of Grief: One Family's Journey to Healing After the Tragic Death of a Son*, page 28.
5. *Life After Loss: Conquering Grief and Finding Hope*, page 56.

suicide or accidental death. The death statistics in this section, however, are not included to paint a grim outlook. They are included to acknowledge the simple fact that people die. On the other hand, many more people continue to live and, therefore, have the opportunity to tell loved ones how they feel.

With Loving Letters, we can rejoice in our love and appreciation for others by sharing it with them instead of keeping it to ourselves. The purpose of this book is to provide a process for and encourage people to write Loving Letters to people they love, appreciate and value – now; while they are still with us and while we can enjoy the many benefits of such communication. Those benefits are addressed in the following chapters.

Important Points

•> Letting loved ones know how we feel about them is far too important to put off.

•> We can avoid possible regrets of things left unsaid by communicating with loved ones while they are living and before it's too late.

•> We can rejoice in the love and appreciation we have for others by openly sharing it with them.

One More Day
By Lilia Fallgatter

If I had just one more day with you
I'd change how things played out
The words that I last spoke
Would not leave a single doubt

Did I say how much you meant to me
And how you changed my life
That my world was much more beautiful
With you standing by my side

One more day would mean so very much
It hurts me not to know
If you knew how much I cared for you
Why did you have to go?

To be sure you know what is in my heart
I'll put it in a letter
Fly it up to you on Angels wings
Send my love and say a prayer

And though you can't write back just now
My faith will have to do
Since I know that you are in good hands
Now that God is holding you.

3.

Beyond "I Love You"

In the movie *It's A Wonderful Life*,[6] the (suicidal) main character, George Bailey, gets to experience what life would have been like for those he loved if he had never been born. His brother would have drowned at a young age – because George was not there; his mother would have been left childless after losing her only son in a drowning – because George was not there; his wife would have never married – because George was not there; and the druggist would have likely killed someone by incorrectly filling a prescription – because George was not there. He was not there, because he never existed.

The message this movie so poignantly drives home is this: **No matter who we are, by our very existence, we impact the lives of others.** If a child is born and lives for only minutes on this earth, that child will affect the lives of

---

6. Liberty Films, RKO Radio Pictures Inc. (1946)

others, in spite of his short life. No one enters this world, for even a second, without having had an impact on other souls. By our very being, we have an effect.

Unlike George Bailey, we will never actually get to "see" what effect we have had on the lives of those around us. And unless they tell us, we may never "know." One thing is certain; we do know what impact others have had on us. Someone in your life may have actually had a profound effect on the person you are and the life you lead today. Perhaps something they said or did changed your direction or path in life. Only you know how their words or deeds affected you and what their presence in your life has meant to you. Therefore, only you can tell them.

We know whom we care about and why we care about them. The question is: Do those we love know we love them? If we have never told them, how could they possibly know? Even if they know we love them, do they know why? If not, how can we tell them? Is saying "I love you" enough to convey what they really mean to us?

"I Love You" Is Not Enough

One of the most common ways used to express that we care for someone is by saying "I love you." Those three simple words that mean a lot to many people (yet can be intimidating to some) are used to convey the message that we care deeply for someone. Just saying I love you, however, is not enough to let them know how we really feel. Why? Because those three words, although they can pack a powerful punch, are inherently vague. They do not express WHY we love someone. Why do you love a particular person?

14

What is it about that person that makes them a special person in your life? Did they overlook your flaws and love you unconditionally? Have they somehow made your life easier, happier and more interesting? Have they taught you about yourself, about life or about love? If so, why not tell them?

It's In The Details

When we say or write the words "I love you" to someone, the person may get the general idea that we care about them, but still not know why. To more specifically convey our feelings about them we must detail the reasons. Thus, in my view at least, a good companion to Elizabeth Barrett Browning's beautiful poem which begins *"How do I Love Thee, Let Me Count the Ways"* might have been a poem titled *"Why Do I Love Thee . . . ."*

Telling loved ones that we love them is great. Letting them know why we love them is even better, because it will be more meaningful to them. Providing specific details and concrete examples can go far in truly letting them know what they mean to us. However, we live in a society where openly expressing our feelings for someone (except perhaps in a romantic setting) is not very common. Sitting down face-to-face with someone to tell them we love them and detailing why we love them is not something people generally do. Doing so could be awkward and uncomfortable.

Thus, the solution and best option, for the many reasons explained in the next chapter, is to tell loved ones how we feel about them in a Loving Letter.

Who Do You Love?

As our lives change, so do our relationships with family and friends. Relationships may be affected by changes in age, employment, distance, marital status, and family situation. I believe that people are in our lives for a reason. They serve a purpose in our lives and we in theirs. We meet when we are supposed to meet and then go our separate ways following our individual paths in life.

Who are the people in your life that mean the most to you? The people that mean the most to you may surround you daily or frequently. Some you may see or speak to only occasionally. Others you may no longer see or communicate with at all.

The people who have touched our lives or had an influence or significant impact on us (either over a period of time or in an instant) have left an imprint that neither time, nor distance or lack of communication can erase. Whether a parent, sibling, grandparent, aunt, uncle, cousin, niece, nephew, friend, teacher, supervisor, priest/pastor or total stranger, at every stage in life, we are affected by and learn from those around us. They may have guided our path, offered advice and support, or somehow came through for us in a crisis.

The people who have had a positive influence in our lives can be fairly significant in number. A simple way to confirm this, is to give yourself five minutes in which to list the names of the people you care about which come to mind in that time period. Over time, the list will continue to grow and may also serve as your checklist of people to whom you wish to write Loving Letters.

The people we care about and who have had a positive

16

impact on us DESERVE to know what they and or their actions have meant to us. By acknowledging sacrifices or acts of kindness, great and small, we honor them. A Loving Letter provides a means by which to honor those you love or appreciate. It is a permanent record that they existed and were valued by another. It is proof that you cared enough to put it in writing.

Important Points

● No matter who we are, by our very existence, we impact the lives of others.

● The words "I love you" are inherently vague. To specifically convey our feelings we must detail the reasons.

● A Loving Letter constitutes a permanent record that the person existed and was loved by another.

4.

The "Write" Solution

As noted in Chapter 1, a Loving Letter is a letter written to someone we love telling them how we feel about them and why. I call this type of letter a "Loving" and not a "Love" letter because although the letter expresses loving sentiments, the phrase "love letter" is generally associated with romantic love. A Loving Letter, just as its name implies, is a letter expressing loving sentiments. It can be, but is not necessarily, romantic. It can be written to anyone we care about and can be written at any time and for any reason. The process for how to write a Loving Letter is detailed in Chapters 7 and 8.

It's The "Write" Thing To Do

One of the easiest, yet most powerful, tools we can use to express our feelings for others is through writing. Writing symbolizes the act of pouring our heart and mind onto the blank page, with our hand serving as the conduit to its creation.

Writing, as a form of communicating our feelings to others, serves many important purposes.

- Writing out thoughts and feelings allows us to **avoid any awkwardness** that might occur if we were expressing our feelings to someone face-to-face. Writing allows us to express intimate thoughts while in the privacy of our own thoughts.

- Writing allows us time to fully think through what we want to write. It also allows us to review and change or **edit** what we wrote until we are satisfied that the words accurately reflect the message we wish to convey. When we express ourselves verbally, editing is not an option. Even if we try to take back or rephrase what was said, it is already "out there," and has been heard and absorbed by the listener.

- According to experts, writing can have **therapeutic** effects. Indeed, there are books and web sites espousing the benefits of writing as therapy. They reveal that writing therapy may include letter writing, journal writing and even poetry writing. It is interesting to note that, although journaling may be

20

considered a relatively recent trend, some people have been journaling (or writing in diaries) for years and can attest to the benefits of doing so. The sheer popularity of journaling (books and programs abound) speaks for itself.

•❖ A Loving Letter may become a **treasured keepsake** of the recipient. For various reasons, our written words may resound and remain (both physically and emotionally) with the person for whom they were written. When thoughts are written, they take a physical form and become tangible. Though spoken words may be quickly forgotten, the written word is something the person we gave it to can revisit. They may relive the good feelings they had when they read it for the first time and savor those positive emotions each time they read it (and long after having read it for the first time.) Also, the letter may be handed down from one generation to the next as a family heirloom.

•❖ Written words may also constitute a **great kindness** to the person to whom they are directed. More on this point later.

•❖ The recipient of a loving letter may **"hear" the message** more clearly when it is in writing. When we communicate with someone

21

verbally, the person to whom we are speaking may hear our words, but may not listen to the message. When they read our words, we have their undivided attention, as they will read the words in their own voice (mentally or as they speak them aloud.)

Thus, there are truly many benefits to expressing ourselves through the power of the written word.

Good Words

Writing a letter telling people how we feel about them and expressing why they mean so much to us can have a profound impact. What other people think or say about us is important. From a young age, into adolescence and through adulthood, we seek approval from and want to be well regarded by others. Being liked and accepted can play an important role in how we conduct ourselves and our lives. It can affect what actions we take and the decisions we make in life.

The importance of what others think about us, and the potential this information has for affecting us, was demonstrated in a letter that appeared in the *Dear Abby* column in December 1997. The letter told of an assignment a teacher had given to students, which required them to write something nice about each of their classmates. The teacher compiled a "list" of the comments made about each student and gave each their list to keep.

Several years later, the teacher attended the funeral of one of the students who had been in the class and who had died in Vietnam. She was touched to learn from his parents, that he had been carrying with him the "list" of comments compiled all those years before. The teacher also learned from many of his classmates, that they too had kept their lists, and kept them tucked away in a special place. Abby's response included a quote from English Poet George Herbert: "Good words are worth much, and cost little."[7]

The quote Abby included in her response is directly on point and captures the essence of the tremendous effect words (in this case – a written list) can have on a person. Without intending to do so, the teacher created lists that became the paper treasures of those who received them. The lists meant so much to the students that many of them either carried them around or kept them in a safe place. Long after they had been written, the words were still significant and highly valued by the recipients.

By writing "good words" to those we love, the people receiving them are permitted to view themselves from a completely different perspective – our perspective.

Through our words, they can see themselves in a different light. They may see themselves in a way in which they may have never seen themselves before; as people considered to be helpful, supportive, creative, or inspiring to others. Our words may serve as validation that they are truly loved and that they mean something to someone. Our words may acknowledge or reinforce the fact that they are deeply cared for, needed and valued.

Several years ago, when I was a young law student and experiencing a difficult time, I received letters from two people. Those letters contained "good words." In their

---

7. George Herbert, 1593 - 1633

letters to me, these individuals described how they viewed me, the kind of person they thought I was, offered encouragement, and highlighted what they believed were my best qualities. Their good words meant a lot to me. They arrived at a critical time and played a crucial part in how I decided to view and handle the situation in which I found myself. I saved those letters because they were encouraging and uplifting. I keep them tucked away and have re-read them several times over the years. Long after the pain of a difficult and challenging time has dissipated, those words still mean a lot. Without any intention on the part of the authors of the letters, their words have become my treasured keepsakes. As a result, without knowing they were doing so, the persons who wrote those letters performed a great kindness in providing much needed support and long lasting encouragement.

Reconnecting

A Loving Letter may serve to strengthen or re-establish a bond with someone we care about, but with whom we may have lost touch. During the course of our lives we may lose contact with people who mean a lot to us. Whether we lose touch due to physical distance, growing apart or a falling out, once we lose contact with people we care about, it may not be easy to reconnect with them. Your good words to someone who matters to you, but with whom you have not spoken in years, may serve to rekindle an old or long lost relationship. Reconnecting with those individuals may fill a void or bring closure where it is needed.

Good words <u>do</u> cost little. In fact, with the possible nominal cost of paper and ink, good words cost nothing. The only expenditure is in the form of the time and effort put forth in writing them. Yet, this simple act can go a long way and may indeed constitute a great kindness to the person receiving them. Through "good words," we may unwittingly benefit others.

I believe that loving others and being loved by others are the heart of the purpose of human existence. Loving Letters are written testimony that such love not only existed, but was communicated.

Important Points

• Communicating feelings in writing serves many purposes: avoids awkwardness, allows us to edit our writing, may be therapeutic, allows us to create a treasured keepsake and may constitute a great kindness.

• Good words really <u>are</u> worth much and really <u>do</u> cost little.

• Good words enable others to view themselves from a different perspective.

• Good words may help re-establish or strengthen bonds.

26

5.

A Lost Art

In an age where technology takes a front row seat in nearly everything we do to communicate with others, perhaps something important has been lost in the process of using those methods.

E-Mail

The most common and highly popular method we use to communicate with others in writing is by electronic mail. Why wouldn't e-mail be so popular? It offers numerous benefits associated with convenience of use and easy access. It allows us to communicate with others more quickly and more often than we might otherwise. Despite the benefits, however, there are some disadvantages to using it. Among them, is that e-mail is easily disposable. E-mail messages are not something most people keep. The delete function is just one click away and with the touch of one button, we can quickly and easily clear away any and all messages to make room for more. Another disadvantage is that e-mail is typically used to communicate with loved ones in a casual and informal way. Using such an informal and possibly non-secure method of communication makes it difficult to effectively approach the serious and personal topic of how you feel about someone. Also, though we write the content of the message, because the communication is electronic and our hand never makes contact with paper, it somehow seems cold and impersonal. Letters, on the other hand, are three-dimensional and tangible. In addition, letters that are handwritten convey a sense of intimacy.

Greeting Cards

Another common method of communicating with loved ones in writing is through the use of greeting cards. According to the American Greeting Card Association[8], there are an estimated 3000 greeting card publishers today, compared with just 100 in 1941. Clearly, there would not be as many publishers if the demand for the product did not exist. This, along with the introduction of e-mail may account for, at least in part, the lost art of letter writing.

Other greeting card statistics of note:

- Over 90 percent of U.S. households buy 1 card per year.

---

8. *See* www.greetingcard.org.

- The average U.S. household buys 35 individual cards per year.

- The average card retails for $2 to $4.

- The industry generates more than 7.5 billion dollars in annual retail sales.

Why are greeting cards so popular? Like e-mail, greeting cards are convenient and take the work out of communicating with those we love. As an average consumer, I buy several greeting cards each year. Like most people, I go to the store; read several cards until I find one I like and which I feel reflects what I want to say to the person for whom I am buying the card; I pay for it; write a short note; sign my name; and deliver or mail it. With the possible exception of sending an e-card, there is nothing simpler.

Although greeting cards are a convenient way to show people we care or to let them know we are thinking of them, a greeting card alone is not enough to effectively convey our feelings for someone. I am not suggesting that greeting cards cannot be used in expressing our personal feelings to loved ones. But there should be more to the communication than pre-printed words written by someone else. Consider your own experience. Have you kept every greeting card you have ever received? Based on informal surveys conducted in workshops and personal experience, I would venture to say that most people keep some, but not all, of the cards they receive. The reasons why people don't keep greeting cards (that on the average cost the sender

29

anywhere from two to four dollars) may be as varied as the individuals receiving them. However, no matter how beautiful the card and how touching or inspiring the pre-written sentiments, you did not think of them and you did not write them. Therefore, they simply don't mean as much to the recipient.

The page that follows contains two greeting card samples. The first card includes the name of the recipient and is signed by the sender, while the second card includes a personal note in addition to the signature. The first card can be likened to receiving a form letter. Except for the name at the top and signature at the bottom, there is nothing to distinguish it from any other greeting card. The personal message in the second card is what makes it unique. It reflects thought and effort put forth by the sender. Put yourself in the shoes of the recipient. Which card would you prefer to receive?

In order for words to have more significance, they must come from you. They must come from your heart and your mind, and be written by you, specifically for that person. It is in expressing our personal sentiments in our very own words that make all the difference. Thus, despite the convenience of e-mail and greeting cards, nothing can replace the power of the personal message and its impact on the recipient.

Sample Greeting Card #1

Dear Andrea,

When the winds of change
Are blowing you away,
Remember -
You always have me
To hang onto.

Love, Gary

This sample shows the inside of a greeting card with the pre-printed message with the recipients' name and sender's signature added. There is no personal message included. Compare this card to the one on the page that follows.

Sample Greeting Card #2

Andrea,

I know life has not been easy for you lately and I really wish I could make everything right again. But in the many years I've known you, I have seen your strength and resilience shine through during the toughest of times. I know you will come out of this a better person.

I'm here for you. Please let me know how I can help.

Love, Gary

When the winds of change
Are blowing you away,
Remember -
You always have me
To hang onto.

This sample shows the inside of the same greeting card as in Sample #1 on the previous page. In this card, however, the sender added a personal message to the recipient. The message, though short, shows that the sender put some thought into communicating his feelings. A comparison of the cards shows the stark difference personalization can make. If you were the recipient, which card would you prefer to receive?

Important Points

●◆ Although there are other methods to communicate with loved ones, which are easier and more convenient than writing a Loving Letter, they may seem impersonal and can be easily discarded.

●◆ In order for written words to have more significance, they must come from you and be written by you for a particular person. It is the personalization that makes all the difference.

6.

Preparing to Write

Writing anything, but especially writing personal thoughts and feelings about someone you care for, takes time, effort and courage. For most people, time is at a premium. Even if you can manage to find some time to write, the thought of putting forth the effort to effectively express how you feel about someone you love can be daunting. Writing a Loving Letter is like wearing your heart on your sleeve; your innermost feelings for someone you care about will become known to that person. Thus, the simple act of revealing your feelings requires working up the courage to do so.

This is where the process for writing a Loving Letter comes in. It involves simple steps to follow in both preparing to write and then in actually writing a Loving Letter.

The processes included in Step 1 focus on exercises that will help develop the content to be included in the letter. The processes in Step 2 focus on the actual writing of the letter. These two steps are designed to facilitate the writing process and make your letter writing experience easier than you might think.

Before delving into the actual writing process, there are some important pre-writing considerations to cover. They are important because they will help prepare you to write.

Setting The Scene

Before you even pick up a pen or pencil, you should consider your environment. Writing a Loving Letter is like creating a work of art; Like any work of art; it requires inspiration. Thus, the goal should be to find or create surroundings that will evoke the inspiration to write. The "right" environment, however, is as unique as each individual.

Some people find peace, comfort and inspiration in nature. To them, climbing to the top of a hill, or sitting under a tree or by the seashore may serve as an ideal setting for writing. Others may find that sitting quietly by a fire or amid the sounds in their favorite coffee shop works best.

It is also possible to "create" an inspiring space for writing in your own home. Some writers may garner inspiration from a comfortable chair, lighted candles, or just being surrounded by their favorite things.

Whatever and wherever the place you choose to do your writing, it is imperative that you are comfortable and able to relax and focus. Noise, interruptions and even slight discomfort are likely to make inspiration elusive. Because your surroundings will affect your writing, creating a setting conducive to letting thoughts and ideas flow easily will work best for producing the desired results.

Avoid interruptions by selecting a time and place where you will not be disturbed by ringing phones, doorbells or other bothersome noises. These distractions can be frustrating and may make it nearly impossible to concentrate.

Finally, make certain your physical environment is comfortable. Seating, lighting and climate all contribute to overall comfort level and should be taken into consideration in choosing or creating your writing environment.

After finding the right space, you may choose to enhance the setting you have chosen or created by using pillows, candles, incense, music or other items that will add to your comfort level.

State of Mind

In order to make the Loving Letter writing experience a successful one, it is also important to be in the appropriate state of mind.

When you have found or created a quiet, comfortable and relaxing environment, take some time to focus on your state of mind. Mental preparation is just as important as any other aspect of preparation. It consists of relaxing your mind and body and then focusing on the subject of the letter. Although the environment contributes to the ability to relax and focus, there must also be a deliberate effort to put yourself in the right state of mind. You can do this by engaging in meditation exercises to clear and quiet your mind, followed by visualization exercises to help you focus on the person to whom you are writing. Meditation and visualization should be undertaken just prior to writing a Loving Letter.

Simple meditation and visualization exercises are included below. These or any similar exercises may be used as you prepare to write.

Meditation

The purpose of engaging in meditation is to clear, settle and prepare your mind. Clearing your mind of any worries will make it easier to concentrate and remain focused on the letter and the person to whom you are writing.

A simple meditation exercise I frequently use involves the following steps:

1. Take several (6 to 9) deep and cleansing breaths. Inhale through your nose and exhale through your mouth.

2. Starting with your head and ending with your feet, focus on relaxing the muscles in each part of your body.

3. In your mind's eye, picture something you find relaxing: perhaps a quiet and breezy beach, a babbling brook or fluffy white clouds rolling across a blue sky.

Visualization

The purpose of visualization is to focus your mind specifically on the person to whom you are writing a Loving Letter.

An exercise I like to use involves picturing (in my mind's eye) the person's face. I focus on their facial features and see them smiling at me. I think about them for a bit before moving on to Step 1 of the letter writing process.

In writing a letter to an old friend, I pictured her lovely face. I could see her beautiful, auburn hair shimmering in the sunlight. She was smiling and I could see her dimple. Her eyes were squinting and I could see her brow furrowing a bit from the brightness of the sun. I thought of what she had meant to me. I thought of how she had always been there for me. This visualization exercise helped me focus on her and made it easier to write my Loving Letter to her.

Meditation and visualization exercises are recommended, but are not absolutely necessary. They are intended to help you relax, focus and unleash your creativity.

After you have created the right environment and achieved the needed state of mind, it is time to move on to Step 1.

Important Points

•❖ Preparing to write a Loving Letter helps facilitate the writing process.

•❖ Writing a Loving Letter is like creating a work of art, and thus, requires inspiration.

•❖ Inspiration may come more easily if you create the proper environment and state of mind.

7.

The Loving Letter
Step One

Writing a Loving Letter can be a wonderfully enlightening experience. Because it requires us to deliberately engage in considering our relationship with the person to whom we are writing, the process of writing the letter may give us new insights into ourselves as well as a loved one. Also, because of the nature of the letter, you (as the author) may experience any number of positive consequences. Writing the letter will provide the opportunity for introspection and evaluation. How often do you get to deliberately contemplate what specific people mean to you? If you are like most people, the answer is rarely. Writing a Loving Letter will allow you the opportunity to do so.

In this chapter, we get down to the serious business of communicating with those we love. If you have taken the steps described in the preceding chapter, you are now prepared to write your letter. As previously noted, the Loving Letter writing process involves two distinct steps.

Each step is detailed below and includes exercises and examples. Before you begin writing, it may help you to read through the description of what each step entails.

Step 1 - The Lists

Step one immediately follows the meditation and visualization exercises described in the section titled *Preparing To Write*. To reiterate, during the meditation, you may first want to relax and clear your mind, then focus on and visualize the person to whom you are writing the letter. As you visualize your loved one's face and see them smiling at you, think about the qualities or characteristics you enjoy or admire in him. Next, follow the directions in Exercise A below.

A. On page 44 or on a separate sheet of paper, create a list of words or phrases that describe the person to whom you are writing.

Information and Resources

- The Appendix on page 95 contains a list titled Descriptive Characteristics. The list may be helpful if you are having trouble getting started. Even if you are not having trouble, it may be helpful to review the list to get a jumpstart on your list. Note that the list included in the Appendix is not an exhaustive list and you are encouraged to add your own if you come up with character-istics which have not been included.

•❖ Chapter 9, page 55, contains a sample list of descriptive characteristics. You may use the sample as a reference in creating your own list. It is included only to give you an idea as to what a list might look like. Keep in mind, however, that there is no specific order or format for creating the list.

•❖ Below are questions that may help to trigger ideas of items to include in your list.

1. Are there specific characteristics that you identify or associate with the person to whom you are writing?

2. If you had to describe your loved one to someone who did not know her, what would you say?

Descriptive Characteristics

_____

_____

_____

_____

_____

_____

_____

_____

_____

_____

_____

_____

_____

_____

_____

_____

_____

_____

_____

_____

_____

_____

When you have completed this list, move on to Exercise B of Step 1 on the next page.

B. On the next page, or on a separate sheet of paper, create a list of memories or significant occasions and events you have shared with your loved one.

Information and Resources

●● Chapter 9, page 56, contains a sample list of memorable events/occasions. It is included as a reference for creating your own list. Again, keep in mind that there is no specific order or format for creating the list.

●● Below are questions that may help to trigger ideas of items to include in your list.

1. How do you know your loved one? When and how did you meet?

2. What are your favorite memories of time spent with your loved one?

Memories and Events

_____

_____

_____

_____

_____

_____

_____

_____

_____

_____

_____

_____

_____

_____

_____

_____

_____

_____

_____

_____

_____

_____

_____

Once the list is completed, take it and the list of descriptive characteristics completed in Exercise A, and move on to Step 2 in the next chapter.

Important Points

•❖ Writing a Loving Letter allows us to gain new insights to ourselves and our relationships with loved ones.

•❖ Creating lists of a loved one's characteristics and memorable events shared with them are key factors in facilitating development of the content for a Loving Letter.

•❖ Answering the questions included in this section, as well as utilizing the resources included, will assist in writing the letter.

8.

The Loving Letter
Step Two

Chapter 7 covered Step 1 in the process of writing a Loving Letter. The exercises included in Step 1 are the equivalent of a brainstorming session, where you developed ideas for the content of your letter in the form of lists. Step 2 in the process is covered in this chapter. It is intended to guide you from producing the initial draft through producing the final draft of the letter. Using the lists compiled in Step 1, Step 2 includes exercises for writing the first draft, editing the first draft to create the second draft and then producing the finished letter. As you draft your Loving Letter, keep in mind, unlike a business letter, there is no specific format to follow. Following Step 2, samples of a first, second and final drafts of Loving Letters are included for reference in Chapter 9.

Step 2 – The Letter

With lists in hand, you are now ready to begin writing the letter.

A. Write the first draft: Using the lists you created in Step 1 as a guide, write the first draft of the letter to your loved one.

- ◆ Refer to and try to incorporate most, if not all, of the items on the lists. These need not be in any particular order or format.

- ◆ At this point, there is no need to worry about editing your writing or organizing the contents. The focus should be on getting thoughts down on paper.

- ◆ Keep in mind that when you are expressing genuine feelings in writing, there is no right or wrong way to do it. What you say and how you say it is completely up to you. If you don't like what you wrote, you can simply try again.

B. Write the second draft: Review and edit the first draft of the letter. Then re-write the letter with the changes you made in the editing process.

- ◆ Check the letter against the lists to be sure you included all the items you wanted to include.

●◆ Make any grammatical and style changes.

●◆ Incorporate any other items such as poetry, inspirational quotes or phrases you want to include.

C. Write the final draft: Review and edit the second draft of the letter to create the finished draft.

●◆ Make corrections and incorporate any other information you wish to add.

●◆ Chapter 10 provides information on putting final touches on your letter.

Important Points

- ❦ Each step in drafting a Loving Letter plays an important part in helping to create your letter.

- ❦ When it comes to the content of Loving Letters, there is no right or wrong. Each is a unique work of art.

9.

Samples

A Letter To Mandy

I met my friend Mandy in high school. Although I had seen Mandy around in junior high school, our paths had never crossed and I did not really know her until we became friends in 9th grade. Our meeting must have been uneventful because, for the life of me, I can't remember how we met or how we became friends. I do remember that Mandy came into my life at a crucial time, having lost my then best friend due to circumstances not of our own doing. I was at loose ends and without a best friend during this important transition to high school.

Mandy was different from most of the friends I had had until then. Although we were of similar socio-economic backgrounds, she was of a different ethnic background. Her family ate different foods, played different games and, in general, lived very differently from my own family. Despite the differences, however, our values and beliefs were very much alike. It was through those values that we formed what for me became an extraordinary and significant relationship.

A few years after high school, our lives began to take us in different directions and our communication became less frequent. Although we each made an effort to stay in touch and saw each other a few times over the years, eventually we did lose touch. Despite that, Mandy has remained an important figure to me. She taught me important lessons about life and especially friendship, which I continue to value and hold close to my heart.

The pages that follow contain lists and letters like those described in Chapters 7 and 8, which I created in writing a letter to my friend Mandy. These samples are included to demonstrate the process for writing a Loving Letter.

Sample List – Descriptive Characteristics

Honest

Caring

Thoughtful

Considerate

Fun-loving

Funny - Self-deprecating

Quirky

Loyal

Beautiful - inside and out

Notes: The words listed above are the words that come to mind when I think of my friend Mandy. They represent the characteristics I associate with and which I would use to describe Mandy to another person.

Sample List – Memories and Events

Driving/cruising

Eating -

    School lunches

       Chili Cheese dogs and Chili Fries

Nightclubs, Disco & Fake IDs

Drive-in movies

Mini-Golf

Friday night football games

Senior Trip -

    First and only (ever) fight

Senior ditch day at the park

Senior Prom

Fireworks!!

Notes: In the list above, I included memories and events that immediately came to mind when I thought of my friend Mandy. They are memories/events I associate with her, which represent of our friendship.

Sample Letter - First Draft

Mandy,

When we first became friends, I was struck by how pretty you were. I had never had a friend with bright blue eyes and blondish hair before. As our friendship flourished, I learned that you were beautiful on the inside too.

You proved to be caring, thoughtful and considerate. Remember when my then boyfriend went off to boot-camp, and you, Diane and Linda tried to cheer me up by putting on a "private" fireworks display, followed by a game of mini-golf? Boy was that an adventure!

Thinking of you and our many adventures together makes me smile. I especially remember standing by the rails on the second floor of the school, eating hamburgers with fries tucked inside, Friday night football games, the senior ditch day when we went to the park and nearly got caught, the senior prom, going to the drive-in theater, cruising

Speedway and eating chili cheese dogs and
chili fries .

I still remember the bright orange car
you drove. And how you hated to sneeze while
you were driving 'cause you thought it would
make you crash.

Remember our senior trip when we had
our first fight? I hurt your feelings by saying
you were selfish and later apologized.

You showed me what it meant to be a
friend. Your friendship taught me much, and I
value the lessons learned back then.

Thank you.

All my love,

*Notes: Before writing this first draft, I reviewed my lists. I
then jotted down any random thoughts that came to mind about
things I wanted to say (which were triggered by the lists). I
organized those thoughts into the first draft.*

Sample Letter - Second Draft

Dear Mandy,

When we first became friends, I was struck by how pretty you were. I had never had a friend with bright blue eyes and blondish hair before. As our friendship flourished, I learned that you were beautiful on the inside too.

A kind and gentle spirit, you proved to be caring, thoughtful and considerate. Remember when my boyfriend went off to boot-camp, and you, Diane and Linda tried to cheer me up by putting on a "private" fireworks display, followed by a game of mini-golf? Boy was that an adventure! (Not to mention probably a violation of city and state codes.)

Thinking of you and our many adventures together as teenagers growing up in the 70's, makes me smile. I especially remember- standing by the rails on the second floor of the school, eating hamburgers with fries tucked inside (because they tasted better that way), going to Friday night football games, the senior ditch day when we went to the park and nearly got caught, going to the senior prom, going to the drive-in theater, cruising Speedway, eating chili cheese dogs and chili fries and going to discos using our sisters' Ids.

I still remember the bright orange car you drove. I can't sneeze while driving without thinking of you. You hated to sneeze while you were driving 'cause you thought you would crash.

Remember our senior trip when we had our first fight? Actually, it was more of a heated discussion than a real fight. I hurt your feelings by saying you were selfish and I later apologized.

As my friend, you gave me so much of yourself and showed me what it meant to be a friend. Though our lives have taken us down different pathes and we have lost touch with each other over the years,, I want to thank you for being such a loyal and supportive friend during those important years. Your

friendship taught me much, and I continue to
value the lessons learned back then.

Thanks you for being my friend.

All my love,

Notes: When I finished writing the first draft, I reviewed it
and corrected the problems I saw. I reviewed the lists to see if I
had missed anything I wanted to include. My main concern was
to ensure that the messages I wanted to convey were clear and
flowed easily. Those changes/corrections resulted in this second
draft.

Sample Letter - Final Draft

Dear Mandy,

    I don't think I ever told you that it was because of you that I learned the true meaning and value of friendship.

    When we first became friends, I was struck by how pretty you were. I had never had a close friend with bright blue eyes and blondish hair before. As our friendship flourished, I learned that you were beautiful on the inside too.

    A kind and gentle spirit, you proved to be caring, thoughtful and considerate. Remember when my boyfriend went off to boot-camp, and you, Diane and Linda tried to cheer me up by putting on a "private" fireworks display, followed by a game of mini-golf? Boy was that an adventure! (Not to mention probably a violation of city and state codes.)

    Thinking of you and our many adventures together as teenagers growing up in the 70's, makes me smile. I especially remember how much fun we had doing simple things like standing by the rails on the second floor of the school waiting for the cute boys to walk by, eating hamburgers with fries tucked inside (because they tasted better that way), going to Friday night football games, senior ditch day when we went to the park and nearly got caught, going to the senior prom, going to the drive-in theater, cruising Speedway, eating chili cheese dogs and chili fries and going to discos using our sisters' IDs.

I still remember the bright orange car you drove. I can't sneeze while driving without thinking of you. You hated to sneeze while you were driving 'cause you thought you would crash!

Who could forget our senior trip when we had our first (and only ever) fight? Actually, it was more of a heated discussion than a real fight. I hurt your feelings by saying you were selfish and I later apologized.

As my friend, you gave so much of yourself and showed me the meaning of friendship. I want to thank you for the gifts you gave in being loyal and supportive during those important (impressionable) years.

Though our lives have taken us down different paths, I will always hold you close to my heart.   Your friendship taught me much, and I continue to value the lessons learned.

Thank you for being my friend.

All my love,

Notes: This final draft was the result of a review and additional changes I made to the second draft. Upon re-reading this draft I felt I had communicated what I wanted to say.

10.

Final Touches

Now that you have finished writing your letter and you are certain that it says what you want to say, consider adding some final touches. Although the aesthetics are not as important as the content of the letter, they may contribute to its uniqueness and to how the letter is perceived by the recipient.

Appearance and Presentation

Factors to consider for purposes of appearance and presentation of the letter include:

- ❧ The kind of **paper** will you use.

- ❧ The type of **writing** will you use.

➡ How it will be **presented**.

➡ How it will be **delivered**.

Paper options for the final draft of the letter include use of plain paper or special paper/stationery. What you write on, however, is not as important as what you write. Whether you are handwriting or typing your letter on a personal computer, there is a wide variety of paper available at office supply or specialty stores. You may choose to write on personalized stationery or other paper that is special to you.

Options for writing include handwriting your letter or typing and printing your letter using a word processing program on a PC. The first draft should be written in your own handwriting. There is something about putting pen to paper that makes the act of writing more personal than using a keyboard. It's as if you're pouring your heart onto the page through your fingers. Handwriting also somehow seems to contribute to the flow of creativity. If your final draft is to be handwritten, be sure that it is easy to read. If it is to be produced on a computer, you will have a large selection of fonts from which to choose. If you can write calligraphy, you may choose the formal route instead.

The letter may be presented in a number of ways. A wide variety of options exist, with choices ranging from sealing it in a standard envelope or enclosing it in a greeting card, to making it into a scroll tied with a ribbon or presenting it in a gift box.

For purposes of delivery, you may choose to deliver the

letter personally or through the many courier or mail service options available.

It is important to note that when it comes to paper, writing, presentation and delivery, no one choice is better than the next. Choose the options that work best for you and reflect your intentions.

Enhancing Your Message

The message included in a Loving Letter to someone you care about can be enhanced in many ways. You may choose to include a relevant biblical verse, a favorite poem, a beautiful prayer, song lyrics or a quote from classic literature. These, along with the list of books included in Chapter 14, may be used not only as a source of inspiration, but to enrich the message you want to convey.

Another means by which to enhance messages to loved ones is by including personal mementos or keepsakes, such as old photographs, a pressed flower, or an old concert or movie ticket stub with your letter. These personal items not only significantly add to the message but, may give the recipient something more to treasure in addition to the letter. Locating such items may be challenging, but worthwhile.

Scrapbooking has skyrocketed in popularity over the last several years and provides another method for presenting a Loving Letter and special keepsakes we may want to include. In addition to the creativity that goes into writing the letter, presenting the letter as a scrapbook page allows us to be even more creative. Keep in mind, however, that the goal is to communicate how we feel about the person and why we feel that way. Thus, added personal touches should not overwhelm, detract from or obscure the message. The focus of the scrapbook page should be the letter.

I included my letter to my friend, Mandy, on a scrapbook page which featured my Loving Letter to her. Along with the letter, I included two small photos of the two of us, taken during those high school years. I also included three quotes about the meaning of friendship. I felt those items complemented the contents of the letter, which was the focal point of the scrapbook page.

Important Points

● When it comes to writing, paper, presentation and delivery, choose the options that work best for you and reflect your intentions.

● Personal items or added touches included with a Loving Letter should complement and enhance the message.

11.

Finding the Words

At one time or another, you may have heard someone say: "There are no words to express how I feel." What that statement really means is that the person cannot, at the moment, think of the words that communicate exactly how or what he is feeling.

Finding the right words to express how we feel about someone we care for may not come easily. If that is the case as you sit down to write your Loving Letter, don't let that stop you. There are methods you may use to break through writer's block (real or perceived) so that you may find the words you need to effectively express your feelings.

The Lists

The exercises included in Step 1 of the Loving Letter writing process (where you create lists of descriptive characteristics and memorable events) are devised to get thoughts flowing right away. By coming up with specific words and phrases related to the person, without much thought as to how those words will fit together, the task does not seem insurmountable.

Difficult Questions

If you have the lists in hand, but can't seem to begin, there is a somewhat morbid, yet surefire, way to get started. You may contemplate these difficult questions:

- If I were dying, what would I want that person to know? What would I say to them about what they have meant to me and what impact they have had on my life?

- If that person died and I were asked to prepare the eulogy, what would I say about them?

These questions, though difficult, are likely to provoke emotionally charged responses, which will put you in the right state of mind and enable you to express your feelings.

Inspirational Motivation

Sometimes, the words we are searching for may come to us as a result of inspirational reading. Such inspiration can come from a biblical verse, prayers, poetry, song lyrics, classic literature and a variety of other sources. These sources can inspire us to communicate the feelings that arise when we read them. As noted in Chapter 10, these sources may also be used to enhance our message by quoting them in our writing. Chapter 14 includes a list of inspirational books that may serve as resources.

Inspiration to write a Loving Letter may also come from reading another Loving Letter. One of the participants in my workshop, Analilia, sent me the following message:

Dear Lilia:

I was thinking of something to write back to you in reference to the letters I've written to people and the impact they've had not only in their lives, but in mine as well. Since the death of my Dad in February of last year, and as a result of taking your course one month later, things have really changed for me. I no longer take things for granted, and I want those I love to know how much they mean to me.

Analilia went on to say that she had received a letter from her friend, Vanessa, to whom she had written a Loving Letter. Vanessa's letter described how she had been touched by Analilia's letter to her and that it inspired her to write a letter to an old friend.

Like Analilia's letter, writing a Loving Letter to someone could create a chain reaction of letters among friends and relatives.

Preconceived Writing

Another method for finding the words to write to loved ones is through "preconceived writing." This involves engaging in a visualization exercise similar to the one discussed on page 39 of Chapter 6. In this instance, however, after putting yourself in a relaxed state, you are asked to close your eyes and imagine that you have finished writing the letter. In your mind's eye, visualize yourself holding the finished letter and read what it says. Even if you can only imagine reading a portion of the letter, that should be sufficient to get you started in writing the letter.

No matter how challenging it is to find the words to express how we feel about someone may, if we persevere, the words will come.

Important Points

●◆ Finding the words to accurately express our feelings may require answering some difficult questions.

●◆ Finding inspiration to write a Loving Letter may come from any number of sources, including from reading another Loving Letter.

●◆ Visualizing the content of the finished letter may help you to break through writer's block.

12.

A Loving Letter to My Parents

To repeat what I said in the Introduction: "In the course of a lifetime, there are many people who come in and go out of our lives. Some are steadfast in their presence, others fleeting. Each serves a particular purpose or teaches a particular lesson." Although I believe that statement is true, few people have a greater or more significant impact as our parents (or those who serve as parental figures in our lives). A parent, whose sole purpose in that role is to care for, guide, shape and mold a child from infancy to youth and into young adulthood, bears a responsibility incomparable to any other.

Until I had children of my own, I did not grasp the magnitude of what it meant to be a parent. I remember a conversation I had several years ago with my supervisor at work regarding parenting, shortly after the birth of my daughter. I was amused by her comment that "children survive in spite of our parenting." Though I chuckled at her statement at the time, I would later come to realize how much truth there was in it. Having been a parent for more than seven years (hardly a veteran, I know) I have learned that there are indeed many opportunities for parents to mess things up. On the other hand, there are numerous opportunities for parents to get things right.

Although I have always had a great relationship with my parents (not counting the early teenage years), I think it took me nearly 30 years to truly recognize and value what they represented in my life. Luckily, it did not take me another 30 to let them know.

Mom and Dad,

In recent years, I have come to realize that the greatest gift any child can receive is the gift of having loving and caring parents. Though I have taken this gift for granted, I did not want to let another day pass without at least attempting to express my gratitude and appreciation to you both for all you have done for me and all you have been to me.

So much of what is beautiful in my life is due to you. During the course of my lifetime, you have given me the gifts of love, affection, security, stability, protection, sustenance, knowledge, advice, faith and strong values to carry me through.

Your presence, love and support have been constant. From the important firsts—first breath, first words, first bike ride, first tooth I lost and first date—through all of the many significant events in my life (baptism, holy communion, graduations, marriage and the birth of my own children) you have been there for me. Throughout the years, we have celebrated many birthdays, anniversaries and holidays. Some of my most treasured memories are centered on events we enjoyed as a family. My favorite memories are of waking up to "Las Mañanitas" on birthday mornings, helping to make holiday tamales and biscochuelos, and sitting around the kitchen table with family and friends, enjoying good food, while Vicente Fernandez music blared on the stereo.

Thank you for being such excellent role models and teachers. From you I learned the value and importance of many things. You taught me to respect my life and myself by focusing on goals and engaging in activities that would lead to good things. You taught me to respect and accept others for who they are, no matter what their circumstance in life. By example, you taught me the importance of having a strong work ethic. In spite of a lack of means in your own childhoods, you strove toward and worked hard for a better life and succeeded in doing so.

You taught me to take risks. As Mexican immigrants who came to the U.S. with dreams for a better future, you embraced a different culture and way of life, while maintaining love and pride in your heritage. Despite the hardships you encountered, you persevered. You taught me about kindness, compassion, the importance of being of service to others, the value of education and gave me a lifelong love of music. Most importantly, you gave me faith, taught me about the power of prayer and showed me that the most important things in life are people.

Together, you have shared in my joys, hopes and dreams and have been there in difficult times to console and encourage me and provide unconditional love and support.

Thank you for bringing me into this world and for being the loving and caring parents every child deserves.

I love you. God bless and keep you both.

13.

Before It's Too Late

The horrendous attacks that occurred on September 11, 2001, made me aware of something I'll refer to here as "death letters." Death letters are letters written by persons working in professions whose duties may place them in danger of losing their lives. Examples of such professions include firefighters, law enforcement officers and military personnel. The letters are written to loved ones, such as parents, spouses and children, and are to be delivered to them in the event of the individual's death in the line of duty.

A few weeks following the attacks, I was changing the channel on my television, when I came upon a program where the father and wife of a firefighter, who lost his life on 9/11, were reading portions of the letters they were given following his death. As a viewer, it was heartwarming yet heart-wrenching to hear the words he had written to them. It was clear from their reaction, however, that his words to them were meaningful beyond expression. The value of the letters to those left behind was immeasurable and their impact immense.

The concept of the Loving Letter is much the same as that of death letters. The biggest difference, of course, is that a Loving Letter is delivered while the person who wrote it is still living. The purpose is to let those we love, know how we feel about them now—while we and they are still alive. Thus, the Loving Letter might more effectively be called a *Living Letter*. Because it is given to the intended recipient while the author is still living, the Loving Letter communication becomes a shared experience, which may enhance (in even the smallest way) our own life and the lives of those we love.

In Chapter 4, we covered the benefits of putting our thoughts and feelings in writing. One of the greatest benefits of writing Loving Letters is that if, and when, you lose people you love, you can be certain that they knew exactly how much you cared about them and why. You will know for certain that they were aware they had an impact on you and how much they mattered to you. For those reasons alone, a Loving Letter can be invaluable; not just to your loved ones, but to you as well.

The tsunami that occurred in Asia on December 26, 2004, killed over 250 thousand people and left utter devastation in its wake. Similarly, on August 29, 2005, Hurricane Katrina, followed in quick succession by Hurricanes Rita and Wilma, wreaked havoc on the U.S. Gulf Coast, killing hundreds of people and displacing several hundreds of thousands more. In addition, U.S. military action in Iraq has caused loss of life and affected many families whose loved ones have been lost or injured.

The fragility and preciousness of life is brought to the forefront with the occurrence of such events, whether a deliberate act of terror, a destructive force of nature or military action.

Tragic events, such as those noted above, have the effect of forcing us to reflect on our own lives. Interestingly, it seems that when human vulnerability is exposed in this way, we can somehow find the strength to reach out to those around us, whether loved ones or strangers. Amazingly, experiencing or observing tragedy seems to bring out the best in human nature and creates a ray of hope. Hope, which emerges in the form of human kindness and compassion.

Chapter 2 included death statistics for 2002. Over 2.4 million people died in the U.S. that year. That information was included not to instill fear or panic, but to acknowledge that our time here is limited and also to recognize that in light of those statistics, some things in life truly are far too important to put off. Letting loved ones know how you feel about them is one of those things. This was experienced first hand by my sister, Marisa, who participated in one of my workshops. As part of the workshop assignment, Marisa wrote a letter to an uncle who had had a significant, positive impact on her when she was a young girl. Despite the fact that she had written the first draft of the letter, Marisa never quite got around to finishing or mailing the letter. Less than a year later, her uncle passed away – not knowing what he had meant to her. Needless to say, Marisa fervently wished she had finished and sent the letter.

Imagine never having to worry about the possibility that those you loved never knew how you felt about them. As you know by now, you need not imagine it. It is possible.

As George Bailey found out on that cold winter night in Bedford Falls, when you have touched the lives of others in a positive way, the effect of your efforts comes back to you many times over.

This book is not about death and dying, it's about life and living it without regrets that someone we cared about never really knew how much we cared. As previously noted, focusing on death forces us to look at life from a completely different perspective.

Let us go forth, offer good words, honor those we love and touch the lives of those around us – before it's too late.

Important Points

- The Loving Letter communication becomes a shared experience, which may enhance our own life and the lives of those we love.

- One of the greatest benefits of writing Loving Letters is that if, and when, we lose someone we love, we can be certain that the person knew how much we loved them and why.

If I Had To Do It Over

By Lilia Fallgatter

If I had to do it over
I'd tell everyone I love
Just how much they mean to me
That they're gifts from up above

I'd write a Loving Letter
And take time to explain
The difference they made in my life
How their presence eased my pain

If I had to do it over
I would not wait another day
To open up my soul to them
And put it on display

Loving them and being loved
Is a blessing beyond words
It's important that we tell them
While our words can still be heard

14.

Inspirational Resources

Chapters 10 and 11 make reference to ways in which resources can be used to inspire our writing or enhance our messages to loved ones. The purpose of this chapter is to provide a starting point for such resources. The list of resources included here consists of books. However, the inspiration for the "good words" written in Loving Letters may come from a number of sources, printed or electronic. The list is by no means exhaustive and is intended to serve only as a sampling of resources available.

100 Best Loved Poems, Phillip Smith, Dover Publications

101 Great American Poems, Dover Publications

Best Quotations for All Occasions, Lewis Henry, Fawcett

Biblical Quotations for All Occasions: Over 2000 Timeless Quotes from the World's Greatest Source, Stephen J. Lang, Gramercy

The Change-Your-Life Quote Book, Allen Klein, Gramercy

Gathering Pearls, A Treasury of Inspirational Poetry, Susan Marie Jeavons, Virtual Bookworm

Great Love Poems, Shane Weller, Dover Publications

Great Short Poems, Paul Negri, Dover Publications

The Holy Bible

The International Thesaurus of Quotations: Revised Edition, Eugene H. Ehrlich, Collins

The Lift-Your-Spirits Quote Book, Allen Klein, Gramercy

Little Giant Encyclopedia of Inspirational Quotes, Wendy Toliver, Sterling/Chappelle

Love in Verse: Classic Poems of the Heart, Kathleen Blease, Ballantine Books

Lyrics of the Soul: A Collection of Spiritual and Inspirational Poetry; Expressing Love, Self Encouragement and Faith, Le'Juana Searcy, Writers Club Press

The New International Dictionary of Quotations, 2nd Edition, Margaret Miner and Hugh Rawson, Signet

Afterword
John's Legacy

Those who walk uprightly enter into peace; they find rest as they lie in death.

Isaiah 57:2

A few years ago, I met John through my good friend Joanne. She and John later attended my workshop. Shortly before the workshop, I learned from Joanne that John had cancer and had been given a short time to live. I was somewhat concerned and apprehensive about John participating in the workshop, given the subject matter. I realized after the workshop that my apprehension and concern has been for naught. John's presence added a different perspective and allowed him to offer insights that only a person in his position could provide. After all, he was facing certain death. When the workshop ended, John made some complimentary comments about the concept of the workshop and how he thought he and others in his position might benefit from some of the ideas.

John survived more than one and one-half years following his diagnosis before succumbing to the illness. I don't know if John wrote any Loving Letters, but after John's death, I learned from Joanne that prior to his death, John made great efforts to reconcile with some members of his extended family. In the end, it seems that John died having reconciled with those he loved, and hopefully, enjoyed some peace of mind as a result of his efforts.

We can learn a lesson from John, for in the face of death, he had the courage to make things right. We need not be facing death in order to muster our own courage to make the right decisions and make things right in the world.

Appendix
Descriptive Characteristics

A list of descriptive characteristics is included beginning on the next page. It is intended to assist you in completing the list in Chapter 7, Step 1, of the Loving Letter writing process. This list is not exhaustive and you may add any other descriptive terms to it.

Accepting
Adorable
Active
Alluring
Amazing
Ambitious
Analytical
Angelic
Animated
Articulate
Artistic
Assertive
Astonishing
Astounding
Astute
Athletic
Attentive
Attractive
Awesome
Balanced
Bashful
Beautiful
Beloved
Blessed
Brave
Brilliant
Bold
Candid
Capable
Captivating
Careful

Caring
Charming
Chipper
Classy
Clever
Comical
Compassionate
Composed
Conscientious
Considerate
Courageous
Creative
Credible
Cuddly
Curious
Dainty
Daring
Dashing
Dear
Decent
Delicate
Delightful
Deserving
Determined
Devoted
Diligent
Diplomatic
Direct
Disciplined
Distinguished
Discreet

Dynamic
Easygoing
Effective
Efficient
Effortless
Elegant
Eloquent
Enchanting
Encouraging
Energetic
Entertaining
Enthralling
Enthusiastic
Enticing
Ethical
Excellent
Exceptional
Exquisite
Extraordinary
Exuberant
Fabulous
Faithful
Fantastic
Fascinating
Forthright
Frank
Fresh
Friendly
Funny
Generous
Gentle

Genuine
Glamorous
Glowing
Goal Oriented
Good
Gorgeous
Gracious
Great
Happy
Heavenly
Helpful
Heroic
Honest
Honorable
Hopeful
Humane
Humble
Humorous
Impeccable
Incredible
Independent
Indulgent
Industrious
Influential
Informative
Ingenious
Innocent
Innovative
Insightful
Inspiring
Intellectual

Intelligent
Interesting
Intriguing
Introspective
Inventive
Invigorating
Invincible
Inviting
Irresistible
Joyful
Joyous
Judicious
Kind
Knowledgeable
Leader
Lighthearted
Likable
Lively
Logical
Lovable
Lovely
Loving
Loyal
Lucky
Magical
Magnificent
Marvelous
Masterful
Mature
Meticulous
Mindful

Modest
Motivated
Mysterious
Naive
Neat
Neighborly
Nice
Noble
Nurturing
Obliging
Observant
Open
Optimistic
Organized
Original
Outgoing
Outstanding
Partial
Particular
Passionate
Patient
Peaceful
Perceptive
Perfect
Persistent
Phenomenal
Playful
Positive
Powerful
Practical
Pretty

Protective
Proud
Provocative
Pure
Quick-witted
Quiet
Radiant
Realistic
Reasonable
Receptive
Relaxed
Relentless
Reliable
Remarkable
Reserved
Resourceful
Respectful
Respectable
Responsible
Responsive
Righteous
Riotous
Romantic
Sassy
Scholarly
Scrupulous
Seductive
Selective
Self-confident
Self-sufficient
Sensational

Sensible
Sensitive
Sensual
Sentimental
Serene
Settled
Sexy
Sharp
Shy
Significant
Silly
Sincere
Smart
Soothing
Sophisticated
Sparkling
Special
Spiritual
Splashy
Spontaneous
Spunky
Stable
Straightforward
Striking
Strong
Stunning
Stupendous
Suave
Successful
Sunny
Supportive

Sweet
Sympathetic
Tactful
Talkative
Tasteful
Tenacious
Thankful
Thorough
Thoughtful
Tireless
Tolerant
Tough
Traditional
Tranquil
Tremendous
Trendy
True
Trusting
Trustworthy
Truthful
Understanding
Unique
Unpretentious
Unrelenting
Unshakable
Unwavering
Verbose
Vibrant
Vigorous
Visionary
Voluptuous

Vulnerable
Warm
Well-bred
Well-mannered
Wholesome
Wild
Wise
Witty
Wonderful
Worldly
Young
Youthful
Zany

Index

About the Author

Lilia L. Fallgatter is an attorney, adult educator and founder and president of Inspirit Seminars and Inspirit Books, LLC. She holds a bachelor's degree in Public Administration and a Juris Doctorate from the University of Arizona.

As an educator, Lilia has experienced the spectrum of adult education. She has served as dean, education director and education consultant, and has managed various legal and judicial education programs and publications.

In her passion for connecting with others, Lilia devised the process for writing "Loving Letters" to loved ones. Through her workshop, *The Most Important Letter You Will Ever Write,* she has helped others connect with loved ones on a more direct and personal level by letting loved ones know how much they care.

Lilia lives in Chandler, Arizona with her husband and two children. She divides her time between her family and spreading her message – encouraging others to write Loving Letters. She is available for speaking engagements, workshop presentations, consultation and coaching. For more information visit www.lovingletter.com.

To Order Additional Copies

Order copies of *"The Most Important Letter You Will Ever Write,"* online or by mail. Order at www.lovingletter.com. To order by mail, complete and mail this form with payment by check or money order to:

Inspirit Books,
PO Box 13736
Chandler, AZ 85248

(Please Print)

Name:_____

Address_____

City:_____ State:____ Zip:_____

E-mail:_____

The Most Important Letter You Will Ever Write:

Quantity _____ x $11.95* = _____
Tax (AZ Residents only) 7.8% _____
S&H (see below)   _____
                    TOTAL: _____

*Inquire about discounts for bulk orders.

Shipping & Handling: Add $3.95 for first book; add $2.00 for each additional book.

If you have enjoyed this book or if it has had an impact on your life, we would like to hear from you. If you have written Loving Letters you would like to share and/or would like them to be considered for publication, contact us at the above address or online at www.lovingletter.com.

Printed in the United States
64162LVS00001B/155